THE FIRE'S JOURNEY

PART I: INTEGRATION OF THE PARENTS

Printed in the United States of America.

Cover art: Cecilia Yang, *Wing*, 2012. Ink drawing. Copyright © Cecilia Yang. Courtesy of the artist.

A selection of these translations, in earlier forms, first appeared in *Mid-American Review* and *Two Lines*.

Ekiss, Keith, 1968-
Espinoza, Mauricio, 1975-
Odio, Eunice, 1919-1974
Ticas, Sonia P., 1969-

ISBN-13: 978-1-935635-23-9 (paperback)
ISBN-13: 978-1-935635-26-0 (hardcover)
LCCN: 2012952609

FIRST EDITION

98765432 First Printing

TAVERN BOOKS
Portland, Oregon
www.tavernbooks.com

The Fire's Journey

Eunice Odio

PART I: INTEGRATION OF THE PARENTS

Translated by Keith Ekiss

with Sonia P. Ticas and Mauricio Espinoza

TAVERN BOOKS

PORTLAND

CONTENTS

Eunice Odio: An Introduction

Travelers to Costa Rica often depart the capital of San José as soon as they arrive, heading out for the cloud forest of Monteverde, the volcano at Arenal, or the waves at Playa Tamarindo, leaving behind the smell of diesel fumes and the city's concrete architecture. But if you visit the National Theater, a civic treasure modeled on the Paris Opera, you will find a bronze statue guarding the building, the bust of a woman with a fierce, penetrating gaze, and hair of Medusa-like serpents: the mother of Costa Rican verse and the country's most significant international literary presence, *Nuestra Eunice*, as she's been called, the poet Eunice Odio.

At least since 1987, when Óscar Arias won the Nobel Peace Prize for his diplomatic efforts to end Central America's civil wars and decades of political oppression, Costa Rica has been viewed as a kind of "Switzerland of Central America," a relatively prosperous democracy with a high literacy rate and a national health care system, a country known for its commitment to ecology and promotion of eco-tourism. Costa Rica is safe, stable, and de-militarized. But when it comes to the arts, and poetry in particular, English-speaking readers and literary translators have mostly turned their interest elsewhere in Central America, gravitating to the more politically-charged writers of war-torn Nicaragua and El Salvador, to the poetry of Rubén Darío, Ernesto Cardenal, Claribel Alegría, and Roque Dalton.

Eunice Odio's poetry has thus remained almost wholly unknown to readers outside Latin America, obscured on the margins of the region's avant-garde and proletarian-poet traditions. A woman poet who lived a secluded life, Odio was born in a country with, at the time, an antipathy to artists and writers, who often relocated to Mexico City if they wanted to establish themselves as contributors to the vanguard. Odio herself was aware of her marginalized, self-exiled position. Octavio Paz once told her that she was "of that line of poets who invent their own mythology, like Blake, like St.-John Perse, like Ezra Pound; and they are rubbed out, because no one understands them until years or even centuries after their death."

True to Paz's word, Odio's writing has experienced a renaissance since her death in 1974. She is now recognized as the leading Costa Rican poet of the twentieth century for crafting a singular, challenging, and distinguished body of work that draws on currents of *modernismo* and surrealism, while developing a difficult, near-mystical approach to the writing of poetry. Odio's poetry has been translated sporadically (Dudley Fitts first translated her in 1958 for an issue of *New World Writing*; William Carlos Williams translated a poem she wrote about him) and anthologized in a number of collections of Latin American poetry in English. This publication of *The Fire's Journey*, however, marks the first book-length translation into English of any Costa Rican woman poet.

EARLY DAYS AND FIRST BOOKS

Born in 1919 in San José, Odio's independence and devotion to literature were evident from a young age. She claimed she learned to read in a single day at the age of four. At 19, she married, but the relationship dissolved after two and a half years. Odio later wrote that the marriage had one benefit: her husband's family owned a large library where she could spend her free time reading. In the early 1940s, Odio began her career by performing her poems on Costa Rican radio, using the pseudonym Catalina Mariel to conceal her identity as a poet from her family. Her early verse, mostly lullabies, read like tone poems as concerned with sound as with meaning.

> Cascabel,
> cascabelín,
>
> para que duerma el lebrel
> la Luna pone un cojín,
>
> * * *
>
> Rattle
> little rattle
>
> the moon lays down a pillow
> so the greyhound will sleep
>
> — "Sinfonía pequeña" ("Petite Symphony")

As with other Latin American women poets of the time, including

....

Claudia Lars of El Salvador and Gabriela Mistral of Chile, Odio began by working within the tradition of a prescribed "feminine poetics" centered around domestic themes of childhood and the maternal. However, Odio soon began to rebel against this prescription. With her first collection, *Los elementos terrestres* (*Earthly Elements*), Odio crafted a remarkably erotic book-length poetic sequence on the desire for physical and spiritual consummation with an absent lover. Indebted to the poems of the Spanish mystic San Juan de la Cruz and to the *Song of Solomon*, these poems turn the tables on the tradition of idealized love poetry. Odio's poems express the pure physicality of love as much, if not more so, than its emotional dimensions.

Tu cintura en que el día parpadea
llenando con su olor todas las cosas,
Tu decisión de amar,
de súbito,
desembocando inesperado a mi alma,

Tu sexo matinal
en que descansa el borde del mundo
y se dilata.

Ven

Te probaré con alegría.

* * *

Your waist in which the day quivers
filling all things with its scent,
your sudden decision to love

....

as you flow
unforeseen into my soul.

Your morning sex
where the world's edge rests
then lengthens.

Come

I will savor you with joy.

—"Posesión en el sueño" ("Dream Possession")

Los elementos terrestres was published in Guatemala as the winner of the Premio Centroamericano "15 De Septiembre" for 1947, shortly before Costa Rica's brief civil war in 1948. After receiving the award, Odio moved to Guatemala, established citizenship, and never returned to live in her birth country.

Odio published her second collection in 1953, *Zona en territorio del alba* (*Zone in the Territory of Dawn*), a volume that features the early short lyrics as well as occasional verse, addresses to friends, and expansive poems where she began to explore more eclectic, if not outright eccentric, spiritual concerns. Her work became increasingly hermetic, carrying forward the influence of the Mexican writers of the 1920s and 30s known as *Los Contemporáneos*, Xavier Villaurrutia and Carlos Pellicer among them, who countered the socialist realism of post-revolutionary Mexican arts.

During her time spent working for the Guatemalan Ministry of Education, and traveling throughout Central America and Cuba, Odio completed *El tránsito de fuego* (*The Fire's Journey*), a book-length creation myth in four parts which ran to 456 pages on its initial printing in 1957. Peggy von Mayer, the editor of Odio's complete works, describes the poem as a gloss on the opening lines from the Gospel of John: "In the beginning was the Word, and the Word was with God, and the Word was God."

The poem begins in chaos, a proto-world in which time exists but where the material world is just taking shape. A bee speaks, but forgets its name; the male and female spirits of the air are born; they sing, play games, and ask silly questions; wheat begins to grow, cities are nearing; and yet the universe as we know it doesn't yet exist. What world is this? A world in disarray, nearly formless and void, but teeming with a future where "Nothing was foreseen" and yet "All was imminent." This is a world and a poetry of paradox, where the universe is just beginning, where everything is present and yet nothing exists.

Into this world, born of the word that he himself speaks, arrives Ion, the hero of this epic. Named for the rhapsode in the dialogue of the same name by Plato, Ion is the poet as maker, literally. God, in Odio's universe, is a poet. And this is a book with its own spiritual logic, which doesn't conform to any religious dogma, even as it seems to borrow from Catholic and animistic traditions. The elements are just beginning to appear; we're always close to earth and stones. We're never far from the beginning, Odio seems to imply. Creation continues each day. Odio asks for our willingness to experience, rather than explain, this strangeness. Don't look too much for sense and you won't miss it. Consider the poem a speculation, one poet's window into her imagination of the world's unimaginable beginnings, an attempt by a poet to explain the world as the word, as poetry.

LATER YEARS

In 1959, Odio moved to New York City. "The United States scares me," she wrote to her friend and editor, the Venezuelan poet Juan Liscano. Although a "model of social justice" and a "paradise of the proletariat," she concluded that the country was "a highly-polished disaster." She disliked, in particular, the Beats, Pop Art, and feminism. Despite her misgivings, she developed an affection for the country, writing a poem in praise of the Statue of Liberty ("The Bronze Lady"), an elegy for Louis Armstrong, and a tribute to the Hudson River.

Odio changed citizenship again in 1962, settling in Mexico City. She lived among the city's exiles and writers (Juan Rulfo, author of the classic *Pedro Páramo*, was her neighbor and reputed lover) who had moved to Mexico City to escape political oppression in other parts of Latin America. She befriended many painters and published essays on those she admired, among them Leonora Carrington, Remedios Varo, and Frida Kahlo. She continued to write poetry, contributing to literary reviews and compiling her selected poems, published posthumously as *Territorio del alba y otros poemas* (*Territory of Dawn and Other Poems*). Always poor, she made her living by translating (from English) and by writing essays and reviews.

In 1963, she publicly declared her opposition to Communism (in general) and to Fidel Castro (in particular) in an open letter praising the Mexican poet Carlos Pellicer's decision to leave the Communist Party. The letter formed part of a group of articles she wrote criticizing various totalitarian leaders and regimes (she was ecumenical in her dislike of the world's major political powers). In her criticism, Odio furthered her self-imposed exile by alienating herself from the dominant ideology of Mexico's artistic and intellectual community. Always more at home in the spiritual realms, Odio entered the Rosicrucian Order in 1967 where she advanced to the Second Grade Superior of the Temple. Her later poetry becomes increasingly devoted to articulating her unorthodox spiritual visions, culminating in a long ode to her patron saint, the Archangel Michael. She died alone at home on March 23, 1974, her body undiscovered for days after her death, her funeral sparsely attended.

KEITH EKISS
San Francisco, 2012

THE FIRE'S JOURNEY

PART I: INTEGRATION OF THE PARENTS

It's true: But, how
is it true?

Prologue to a Time in Disarray

I

Nothing was foreseen.
All was imminent.

II

One day after a time immemorial
while the sky moved on foot
from eye to eye
thinking itself from heart to heart
in the cities

the order of the void prepared
a word that did not know its name.

(That word was the size of air.)

III

Also, potency renewed, the wind,
uprisen to topple the stars,
rent the burning temples from this thunder

....

I hear without memory
illuminate and count its angels.

IV

Also, a bull, yes, a pale bull
with an earthly face
pounding the world with its heart-shaped hoof.

V

Rivers conjugating, arranging themselves in syllables of water,
confusing the boundaries of fish and fire.

VI

Fruit and children hardly wrote each other
with the ancient stroke that gathered verbs
once free, headless, without a path
on the road of an eternal morning.

VII

Night dreamed its own shape of May.
What would its green be like removed from the leaves?
What would its green be like
beside such a clear design of laurels
rendered in deep petal?

It wished for a word to listen to its color in the night.

VIII

The angels sought a body for weeping,
its lower sex resting in the light
its hair barely the pronoun of waves.

IX

The islands navigated toward a copper town
and ripened their porcelain sun in fishbowls,
but night and day the sand found them
with an ear held to the beehive's door
and their mosses providing an orderly light.

X

Beyond its lullaby, a year away from its beloved viscera,
the harp released its smile, its new bridal beds.

Already it was necessary to arrange its strings
and its stature, grown to the poplar's height;
soon it would meet

its harmonic obligations.

XI

There in its dry age
—with endless memory of snow—
the cold created its childhood.
No one knew if it was a mortal tortoise
or the undated heart of a perennial ring.

Everyone loved it and confused it
with its gold assonance scattered in the desert.

The city full of fresh things already announced it.
One day lightning would come to blow on its shoulders,

a light hurricane would carry it off;

from then on the cold would resound
with those who had forgotten it for centuries
nine sobs of unburied bees ago.

XII

The ocean was only a long presence of horse
around the world

and the horse barely a lip deciphered
and suddenly lost

salt

on the eve of water
weightless and solemn.

XIII

The crystals appointed unanimous customs and measures:
the humble epidote climbed through quartz

....

with its lizard foot;

the rock crystal with its wavering perimeter
shunned contact with the iron
and as it passed through furious flashes

claimed itself unblemished.

XIV

Lambs inside, butterflies inside,
honoring the dust,
showering it with blue conventions and unforeseen beings,
the carnal grace of the cities was emerging.

XV

The bee summarized in its premature virgin's breast
the condensed sweetness of an inexhaustible father.

XVI

It was the first peace that no one repeated.

Soon a great bone began to discover its ear
from morning to bronze, from night to deer.

XVII

It was during the infancy of God,
when he spoke with a single syllable

and continued

to grow in secret.

Integration of the Paternal Element

I

It is said that the earthly object
founded by the event of an absolute word
moves vertebrally sliding endlessly
flowing in quantities of shadow toward the light

until a word the size of air detains it.

II

And a little earth settles. No, it doesn't settle,
rather it forms its pompous apex,
irreproachable;

it comes from a movement
that became a secret guiding fall.

Its space retreats
and perseveres in its plowed dream,
it advances through its eye crowning itself
and rests its natural edge clearly
to seal the declaration of the wheat.

(Afterwards, it's never been known
how it rose to the tongue in the figure of wheat,
when it could become a wing and live sweetly.)

III

In the meantime,
while the sugar rises to its four favorite sides,
an anticipation of air, a gust of insipient gold
opens its color from the snow to the trilling.

From mass to mass,
a fierce breath follows it through all its dominion
from one species to another

from one species to the translucent origin of its order
from the flower to its untransferable cause
according to which the rose

fits only in its diandrous sound
in whose high course a petal announces itself
with the willingness of vigilant silk

quieted and closely contained by the dust,

....

adorned and well-born from afar by the air.

Oh untransferable nature of the rose!
According to which the rose only fits in the rose that surrounds it
more than that other enclosing
the one no one knew;

until at last, multiplied with each day,
secretly discovered by the lip
suddenly divined in memory

it became One,
unpredictable,

rose.

They all ask for her, her back toward them
and know that the rose is the child
in whose skin, through an innocent act,
a bee exchanged its new breast
for the breast of an angel.

IV

A little hardened earth settles, earthly, elemental,
where a young stone pierces through
and weaves with humility the passion it will have
when an eye and a lip detain it
in the sweet word of its name—

let Ion say to he who listens:
It is the stone of all,
stone of the one who names it
in the name of the sacred body I bestow upon it;

my stone

our stone

whose lustrous spume, here on my tongue,
one can hear falling, small and possessed.

V

But the earth does not advance
(such a pale disorder

to speak of the thunder's past order)
because it's expressed in the expansion of a tree

it ascends to the tender curve
without watching it, joyous in its form.

Already it fits on several branches;

serene lengths erected in hyacinth codes
govern its child.

VI

Arriving from its origin,
an unknown brilliance has been released;

behind its movement an immortal

motion

has been born;

—full grace descending through immanent gold
raising it from the shadow with humid potency

....

to spin it in the presence of all metals—.

One sole movement
climbing through its channels toward the naked
and obedient marble;

one more spin

final and divided
and the initial of a thunderous deer,
that semblance of shadow, if blooming,
sprouted in grass and perfected in bleat
the cervine estate,

the first eve, rough and rapid,
of a horned oil and a bifrontal plant.

VII

Thus, from pore to pore,
from arc to arc,
it is covered with solitary species.

Synthesis of the First Exile

I

His musical tremor prepares itself.

Suddenly, morning, crippled among the halos,
imprisoned by a tonal echo and sacred liquids,
a cardial sound has been born to him,
an illuminated shudder.

II

Dust is in the silence of the first solitude,
crippled among the halos,
pasturing among the sacred liquids.

III

Silence!

Let all things converge:

gentle water shall regulate its density
and wine its form;

....

snow shall be the age of whiteness,
the burning poplar shall relent from branch to pure branch.

Let all things be restrained and let joy return to sound.

Silence!

The dust cries out, celestial and crushed by the light,
intimate and emerging, its region surrounded by dawn.

Dust is in the silence of first sounds.

Let great things dream in stone
and small things, lying openly in syllables of lark.

Let time pass blowing toward its final lasting presence

because the imprisoned one

supported by uncertain vastness
by invisible storm wells

powerfully armed by sleep and dark leavening,
gathering his voice and his inherent presence
with the air, without a foot to lead him,

has passed through the Eye of God.

He is present.

Hallelujahs of the First Without Country

I

Hail, oh dust
oh primordial exile
oh heavenly one without country!

II

Let it all be for the heavenly grace of the one without country,
all for his virginal alliance
with pollen unopen to the grace of pollen.

III

Ever since you dwelled with the skyward womb

a drop of flesh

a building raised to its forehead

set down its light foot to take a step.

Oh womb, oh shuddering solitude,

....

oh irate exile of a blushing gust!

With the sound of grain
the bodies go marching

to the city.

Integration of the Parents

I

And the grain mixes with the drop of flesh,
the high provider of touch and hearing
at whose white contact the salts stir
and phosphorous resumes its physical joy.

All neighbors of the flesh
—form, fields of wheat, emptiness—
gather in its vicinity
to nourish the verb-time that matter demands,
the verb of the deep, innumerable child
treading toward the ecstasy of the first movement.

II

In the first movement
a colloid noise endured until it rotated motionless;
and the breath ran beside the nimbus
with the foot of a fixed and endless throne.

The curled pearl undulated forward
and the calm, child-like parents,
feeling for the shining contact,

touched their favorite loving organs.

III

Then

space opened and remained deserted.

A seed blinked
and an eternal eye elapsed.

IV

The bone declined to whiteness
and discovered itself liquid,
flooding its future cavities
and their coming, bitter smells;
but a summer full of fish and mangers
transformed what were merely vestments into solid presence
and a great cycle of paternal flesh was fulfilled.

Infancy of the Parents

I

AIRO
I feel a deep touch of skin below—
but above my forehead

nothing

AIRA
It was me enveloping your touch to the heart

AIRO
A moment ago—long before the flour—
I glanced at you and returned to question

AIRA
You were watching

AIRO
Yes, I was watching you
with what I watch when I weep

not really knowing from which corner of my bones

AIRA

You were your gaze

AIRO

Gaze?

AIRA

You said: watch.

And the gesture joined the firstborn verb
from which the crowned eye emerged

AIRO

So be it

AIRA

My eye is the limit where I end
but I start at another

and climb to possession

AIRO

In which vertebra does it listen?

AIRA

Suddenly it's become silent—
what forehead makes it sink, expressionless?

AIRO

Silent?

AIRA

Silent, final corner, blessed vertex
from where I launch myself toward the first gift
to intimate, tonal architecture

AIRO

Let us be silent

AIRA

Silence, shadow of a thread
where the lip never shadowed itself,
nor the syllable alighted.

I take the risk of leaving by organic leaps,
leaping toward shy, melodious fathers

AIRO

Silent, able the profile, alert the bone,

....

silent on the way to vast dampness

     AIRA
I hear you become silent without me. Your voice
grows at a distance,
a quiet seed of air in your throat

     AIRO
Slow delights overcome me

     AIRA
All is confusion . . .
night begins its successive dreams

     AIRO
My skin receives its cold blind blows

     AIRA
All at once your temple rises and blinks

     AIRO
The sky is becoming taller
The darkness closes

I'm afraid. Your long hair spills

filling me with darkness

    AIRA
Have no fear. The stems darken
assuming the stillness of incomplete beings.

One by one, consuming their share of darkness,
humbling their clear roundness toward the dust,
they await the time of exodus;
exodus toward the light that fits in the alveolus,

alveolus which at dawn celebrates its timid splendor

    AIRO
How do you know the green,
which stays on the clear fruit, won't get lost?

How do you know the spacious air
has taken a path from which it will return bright and habitable?

    AIRA
Rather, the shadow strengthens it

    AIRO
The air may lose its light

....

and tremble, uninhabited,
crossing another realm without depth or shore
and it will be sought in the direction of noon
and no one will find it passing through the sky

AIRA

Don't be afraid. Now the stems darken
but the light and the spacious air
drive their herds toward dawn

CHORUS

Now it's time to sleep.
Another more innocent day will arise
when the lip will speak with its ignorance.

Confusing the foot with the day
and the day with the wheat.

To the wheat it will say: Lord!
and to the dust: crippled angel.

Until one day the fortunate lip
will gather within its walls

the sum of all words

and will utter the sign of joy:

morning

II

AIRA
Today it is daylight everywhere!

My foot dawned with a surrounding light.
Also my hair dawned,

hallelujah!

from such depth,
with the scent of the veins that listen to it

AIRO
Airaaa!

Today is made of wheat . . . linen . . .
it is . . . diurnal

CHORUS
She confuses everything.
Today it is daylight everywhere.
Salt and prophets know this already

AIRA and AIRO
Something I touched without seeing.
Something passed through my ear without touching

AIRA
Perhaps the wind of the Guardian.
He passes suddenly to found the dawn
more swiftly than Himself

AIRO
That suits him as shadow

AIRA
Think no more of the sealed night

AIRO
The day within the air hallelujah!

AIRA
The Guardian will pass another day long before

....

his own speed

and he will not remain hidden

AIRO
Let us sing: thus it is and thus shall it be
and we shall learn of his back in freedom
where warm tensions gather
and temperatures congeal
to found the identity of the air;

his back on which the expanse begins.

Today is daylight and you wear, Aira,
a dress the color of your heart

AIRA
Now that it is day, play at being born,
pretend we were born small,
extend your arms to such clear presence
and let us think about the first poplar;
then we will find it

opened and already foreseen

....

waiting for us

CHORUS

For a long time they awoke without knowing
day was upon the world;
they thought day was the same as dreaming,
they thought to awaken meant to return;
that departing was a thing without light, an absence.

They thought morning meant return, a way of being,
a return without rest
to the entrails of love they couldn't feel.

But one time, being thus, lying about
recalling clearness without being, neither lost nor found,
what never was contained in secret space
nor commemorated in the senses,

suddenly, quieted and ignited,
facing each other, bone against bone,
throat against throat,

through organic steps
through swells of damp and living entrails

....

they entered the primeval roundness.

They gathered their body, their outer joy,

and walking on the foot of dawn
they ascended to their lineage

and spoke the word without shadow;

the word within their reach
waiting only for them to grasp it,

the word meant for all
yet no one had found it:

morning.

And everything fit in her, everything from body and air,
color and wheat;

and everything neither of the body or air,
but of a third species without sound.

And suddenly they spoke the word
knowing themselves the purest:

morning.

All was ready in the world.

All was visible and deep this morning

AIRO
Let us reach the threshold,
give me the hand that lets you clamor to the wind
and play.

One, two,
Three!

The threshold fell from my eyes —blind child—
I was left with the gaze and memory of an island

that once existed where I am now
and stared at itself in the mirror

AIRA
It sailed in the mirror

AIRO
Girl, let's play!

Let's draw the crystal that deceived me this morning,
a crystal that fell from branch to branch growing,
without knowing it was watched, creature of naïve crystal
falling from branch to branch

AIRA

Let's play: my drawing begins in a snail.
The line strikes the numbers of the sand in secret,

don't look at it!

A 2 arrived at the pearls, replacing them
with 2 different sizes from the sea;

2 from a 7 we subtract in the shell:

they are five different candles
losing their leaves in the water

AIRO

My captain!

AIRA

Sir!

....

AIRO
All aboard!

CHORUS
Waves of mint attend the air,
gather one by one,
float by the cool noise of velamen;
fight for each piece of sea spray.
Step by step they trace the detailed
darkness of the wave
and the sailor loses his torso in the lightning

AIRA
My captaaaiiinnn!
The shell's been broken

AIRO
A small shell it was for such great waves.
The angels made a mockery . . .

AIRA
Let us make a shell from mother-of-pearl
that doesn't crumble,
lighter than the wind, great as the water

....

AIRO

I'm tired, it's late, let's draw ourselves tomorrow

AIRA

I will draw you, apple-shaped

AIRO

How much is an angel multiplied by 4?

AIRA

Let us review the multiples of angel

AIRO

Angel multiplied by 4 ... is
governor of 3

multiplied by its own
high and indivisible multiples

raised to inexhaustible power ...
equal to butterfly square.

AIRA

Everything is singing upwards:

the spotted she-bird on her green lemon tree
and the spotted he-bird on his little green branch

AIRO
High, in the tall branch, the orange grows

AIRA
The he-bird sees it

AIRO
The day unravels filaments of dampened violins

AIRA
The he-bird pecks them

AIRO
Wild swallows on the ground begin to bear fruit

AIRA
And the spotted she-bird swings on her branch

AIRO
I went to the sea for oranges,
a thing the sea doesn't have

AIRA

To the sea that goes, coming

AIRO

Give me your hand.
Your little finger isn't my little finger

AIRA

Your little finger escorts me.
I want it for sleeping

and to journey to the country of the grape
with a commanding baton;

a saffron field
marshal's baton;

because your little finger isn't my little finger,
nor your eyes my eyes

CHORUS

Sleep!

AIRA

Nor is my dress the little dress that suits you

....

AIRO
You are a girl

AIRA
The tree that's in the spring,
is it a she-tree or a he-tree?

CHORUS
Sleep!

AIRO
Did you hear that?

AIRA
The star in the tree's
highest branch is speaking.

It passes from spring to branch
and says she came among several sirens
who arrived to the world on holiday . . .

But no one knows it . . .

AIRO
Let's draw ourselves tomorrow

AIRA

I will draw you apple-shaped

Fable of the Bee

I

INTERDREAMISSION

CHORUS
Once upon a time . . .

AIRO
A time

CHORUS
Quiet!

AIRA
Once upon a time . . . quiet! . . . sleep!

AIRO
Quie . . .

AIRA
Fall . . .

CHORUS
A certain time, in spring,
a bee lost her honey returning to the hive.

. . . .

A motionless wind

AIRO
A motionless wind . . . ?

CHORUS
Sleep to my words!

AIRO
To sleep words . . .

> A giant-like child
> came to rest in peace
> all between swaddling
> and signs.

CHORUS
. . . a motionless wind,
a wind barely risen and inhabitable,
took her by the side without harming her.

Soon it said yes, that it wanted her
to speak that yes with many syllables,
and when passing through the salt to only tilt her,
never to reveal her, no, never to reveal her,

....

nor wound her unwoundable peace.

The wind carried her along with its gusts.
There was a light tremor deep within the sky—

meadows and astrolabes
lost limbs, jaspers and geraniums;

the child dropped a wave from his hand.

Then,
a great silence assumed what the wind had left,
added up the facts with numbers of snow

and spoke not a word

II

The bee, having lost her humid efficiency,
—the bee who exchanged her new breast
for the breast of an angel—

retraced with renewed accent
the musical scales that run from the sugar to the spikenard.

It wasn't there.
Where would the youth be, the unnameable one,
the perfumed name that The Guardian
of the hive gave to her?

That which carried her through solid petals
to stamens with the down of archangels?

BEE
Sir, Mister Guardian,
I have forgotten the name that you gave me;
forgive me in the name of the water,
of the bread and the morning.

I have sinned against you, against the deep word,
against the great edified sweetness

THE GUARDIAN
And the wind has carried away what you forgot.
A grave sin it is to forget the names!

While your bee face trembles in fright,
a child purges your sorrow

BEE

A child!
The child with the patience of wings pains me greatly;
pains me there in the wax;
pains me here in the small limbs of my soul

THE GUARDIAN

Somebody must suffer so that your line won't perish

Because of you, hours ago it has been forgotten,
that which you abandoned in your memory.
. . . Everything is confusion in the hive.

They asked for the name, for the word . . .
Nobody knows it.

You should have remembered you are but a spark
of the great golden body,
a vague multiple of the great unity
that nonetheless multiplies in you, begins with you,
grants its virginal impulse to you.

Because of you, instead of anemones, instead of roses,
nightingales will be born!

. . . .

So it is that you, articulate breeze,
you are now the shadow of the honey, the silence of your race,
the abandoned entrails of the flowers.

You forgot the infinite attitude that a single lily assumes,
the light that stems treasure as they grow;

and one by one the parts of the whole are confounded.
Because of you the smiling unity is empty and divided!
Because of you its trembling perfection breaks apart vastly!

Ah, why shouldn't I pass by your face!
If I were to take just one step by your mouth,
I would unravel you forever . . .

But if I burden you,
you won't be able to suffer and find it.

I don't want you to hurt. Be swift.

And yet such a great sin against your race,
a race worthy of the poplars,
must be paid by the trusted one.

While you search, the child must purge

....

the sorrow of a bee.

Only he can endure this nimbus in the flesh.
Only he with his thin patience of wings

    BEE
Watch over his face, Father,
you who are the protector of all things!

    THE GUARDIAN
And who will watch over your wandering face?

    BEE
You have decided it will be the trusted one,
with his long patience of wings

    THE GUARDIAN
Go on! Seek the one who will give you the name,
he knows it long before all things.

His profession is that of mending.

Of placing

a poppy

where the earth descended into darkness

III

CHORUS
From hyacinth to hyacinth she traced the roads.
She got lost looking for a place among the dates;

a place that would reveal her whereabouts
during the past spring;

that silver spring
when the honey lost its garments.

What bee-sorrow
wandered through the meadows last spring!

She no longer has honey on her side
nor fragrance in her seed

and her body is thick, yes, her body is thick,
and the fire at the threshold
of the sad protective alveolus has grown old

IV

BEE
Do you know, my Dardo, do you know the name?

DARDO
We know that name in the past;
petrified, slow, imperfect

BEE
But it's no longer the same. I want an ancient name
in continuous present

DARDO
Nobody knows it here. We have news of it being lost;
but we say nothing. We are already sealed,
soundless, gyrating motionless

BEE
Are you in springtime?

DARDO
We shall remain here
because the man might suddenly remember us

....

and we must surround him at once.
(If not, what terror!)

Everything returns to the point of its absence:
the spheres rejoice in their shape,

the rose moves toward its profile,
May returns to its orbit,
the flax goes inside its stem

But then a new greed consumes he who remembers,
forgetting all the goods that he recalled.

And so the rose is interrupted,
the wine returns to the grape,
I no longer jump;

and everything remains quiet, motionless . . .
Ask the man to remember

BEE
He doesn't hear me. I live in a sound
that leans on his ear without touching it

DARDO

The year's first lark will tell you

BEE

The lark is not here,
but in the spring that's yet to come:
and it was here, in this past spring, where the wind . . .

DARDO

There's no wind in this part of your voyage.
I repeat: we are gyrating motionless.
The wind was entrusted with the coming spring
and has left to go serve it;

now it's moving the frond, carrying the water of time,
in another part of itself

BEE

There in the spring that's yet to come . . .

DARDO

There in the spring that already came

BEE

Do you know it?

DARDO

Everything, the past knows everything,
its empty, sudden inhabitants

BEE

It has returned unraveling mangers and brooks,
surrendering only to its weight of gold!

DARDO

You would be there were you not talking with me now;
the whole of you in a future of leaves and years,
the thighs and the wings engaged in humid works,
wearing a dress fashioned after the poppies

BEE

And the lark, does it know it?

DARDO

Perhaps . . . it was chosen unanimously by the trees.
It must be quite fragrant

BEE

How can I go that far?

DARDO
Far away is the lark in your memory.

You will go riding on lightning
(light opens up inside;
confinement outside)

BEE
And if I fall, who will pick me up?

DARDO
A cloud, standing up, will sustain your breath
and your blond virginal hip

BEE
And if I get lost, who will find me?

DARDO
Morning lamps
with undulating crystal palates

V

BEE
I can hear it like a sound from God

....

LARK

October passes by with its city of leaves

BEE

Can I find in October the maker of all things?

LARK

Thus said the arbor as it sprouted

BEE

I will follow him!

LARK

May you have a good trip through the city of leaves!

BEE

Does the one who knows it live here?

NIMBUS

Ask the Height.
She will give birth to him amid the lightning;

later he will be born in me

BEE

Tell me, Height of the air,
Tell me, presence, longitude of the sky

HEIGHT

I shall birth him after the Expansion

BEE

Will many births light up his flesh?

HEIGHT

Only a successive birth

VI

BEE

Does the maker live here?

THE EXPANSION

He lives, but is not yet born

BEE

Where is the Watchman?

THE EXPANSION
In a place inside me that you already know

BEE
Tell me what you call him

THE EXPANSION
Ion the generator, the beloved

AIRO
I know the child

CHORUS
Silence!

AIRA
We know where his bones are beginning to take form

CHORUS
Nobody will ever know him

AIRA
Stronger than the course of the water is his voice

CHORUS
You will not know him among them all

AIRO
Ion, nobody sleeps, nobody leaves you alone, nobody leaves

BEE
Tell him I come to ask

THE EXPANSION
He will answer nothing

BEE
I come on the word of The Guardian

THE EXPANSION
I would already be wide open
had you first uttered The Name
whose first syllable is my body,
with whose duration I expand eternally, fixed,
my core still, swiftly immobile.

Come in,

so that I can open earth's door to you

....

VII

BEE
I forgot the name
The Guardian of the hive gave to me

ION
Speak of what was forgotten

BEE
It had the attributes of the dew,
the goods and the growth of the morning;

and its color was so rushed that as soon as it began,
over there by the Foot of God, it was consumed
and ended without boundaries.

Its movement was an endless perfume,
its petals were thick and smiling,
high was its moistened fortress

ION
It consumed itself over there, by the Foot of God?

BEE

There it found its end as it began life on earth

ION

There's a place in the air,
a resplendent dominion where whiteness grazes, snowing;

this iridescent hiatus,
this brightness set aside,

its name is white carnation

BEE

I will not sin again

ION

The bees await you.

Everything is confusion in your house.

Go, and tell them that the object, recovered,
is once again identical to itself;

that the key to its body has been returned to you,
whole and possessed forever

BEE
I will go, and will never lose it

ION
May He who watches over everything be with you

BEE
May a physical word from God
be with you, possessor of all things

ACKNOWLEDGMENTS

Many thanks to the editors and staff of the following journals, in which these translations first appeared.

Mid-American Review: "Prologue to a Time in Disarray," "Hallelujahs of the First Without Country"

Two Lines: "Integration of the Parents"

Special thanks to the Santa Fe Art Institute and the Witter Bynner Foundation for their generous support of a Witter Bynner Translators Residency. Special thanks to Rima de Vallbona for her correspondence, Peggy von Mayer for her editorial expertise, and the staff at EUNA.

ABOUT THE AUTHOR

EUNICE ODIO (1919-1974) is considered the leading Costa Rican poet of the twentieth century. She traveled and lived throughout Central America and the United States before settling for much of her life in Mexico City. Her principal works include *Los elementos terrestres* (*Earthly Elements*, 1948), *Zona en territorio del alba* (*Zone in the Territory of Dawn*, 1953), *El tránsito de fuego* (*The Fire's Journey*, 1957), and *Territorio del alba y otros poemas* (*Territory of Dawn and Other Poems*, 1974). In addition to her poetry, she was the author of short stories and numerous political and cultural essays. Her complete works were published by the University of Costa Rica in 1996.

ABOUT THE TRANSLATORS

KEITH EKISS is a former Wallace Stegner Fellow and Jones Lecturer in Poetry at Stanford University and the author of *Pima Road Notebook* (New Issues Poetry & Prose). The past recipient of scholarships and residencies from the Bread Loaf and Squaw Valley Writers' Conferences, Millay Colony for the Arts, and the Petrified Forest National Park, he received the Witter Bynner Translators Residency from the Santa Fe Art Institute for his work on Eunice Odio.

SONIA P. TICAS is Associate Professor of Spanish and Latin American Literature at Linfield College, Oregon. She has published articles on women poets and the development of feminism in El Salvador.

MAURICIO ESPINOZA is a poet and journalist from Costa Rica. He has published a poetry collection, *Nada más que silencio*, articles about literature and the arts, and studies on Latin American literature. He is a Ph.D. candidate at The Ohio State University, researching Latino/a representation in film and comic books.

TAVERN BOOKS

Tavern Books is a 501(c)(3) not-for-profit charitable organization that exists to print, promote, and preserve works of literary vision, to foster a climate of cultural preservation, and to disseminate books in a way that benefits the reading public. In addition to reviving out-of-print books, we publish works in translation from the world's finest poets. We keep our titles in print, honoring the cultural contract between publisher and author, as well as between publisher and public. Our catalog, known as The Living Library, sustains the visions of our authors, ensuring their voices are alive in the social and artistic discourse of our modern era.

THE LIVING LIBRARY

* forthcoming

Tavern Books is funded, in part, by the generosity of philanthropic organizations, public and private institutions, and individual donors.

By supporting Tavern Books and its mission, you enable us to publish the most exciting poets from around the world and revive out-of-print works. Your contribution is essential in our effort to print, promote, and preserve the finest poetry books of our modern era.

MAJOR FUNDING HAS BEEN PROVIDED BY

Lannan Foundation
Lannan

ADDITIONAL FUNDING PROVIDED BY

Dean and Karen Garyet
Dorianne Laux and Joseph Millar
Marjorie Simon
Mark Swartz and Jennifer Jones

To learn more about underwriting Tavern Books titles, please contact us by e-mail: tavernbooks@gmail.com

COLOPHON

This book was designed and typeset by Michael McGriff. The text and titles are set in Garamond, an old-style serif typeface named for the punch-cutter Claude Garamond (c. 1480-1561). Helvetica Neue, used on the cover and title page, is a redesigned and digitized version of Helvetica created in 1983 by D. Stempel AG and Linotype. Printed on archival-quality paper by McNaughton & Gunn, Inc.

In addition to the trade paperback, an edition of 250 hardcovers have been printed. Twenty-six of these are signed and lettered A-Z by Keith Ekiss.